Growing Herbs at Home

A Guide to Growing Herbs At Home for Beginners

By

Charlie Hughes

All attempts have been made to verify the information contained in this book but the author and publisher do not bear any responsibility for errors or omissions. Any perceived negative connotation of any individual, group, or company is purely unintentional. Furthermore, this book is intended as entertainment only and as such, any and all responsibility for actions taken upon reading this book lies with the reader alone and not with the author or publisher. This book is not intended as medical, legal, or business advice and the reader alone holds sole responsibility for any consequences of any actions taken after reading this book. Additionally, it is the reader's responsibility alone and not the author's or publisher's to ensure that all applicable laws and regulations for business practice are adhered to.

Copyright © 2015 by Charlie Hughes

All rights reserved. No part of this publication may be reproduced, distributed, or transmitted in any form or by any means, including photocopying, recording, or other electronic or mechanical methods, without the prior written permission of the publisher, except in the case of brief quotations embodied in critical reviews and certain other noncommercial uses permitted by copyright law.

Table of contents

HISTORY AND USES OF HERBS — 1

Getting started — 4
- Windowsill gardening — 6
- Balcony or roof terrace gardening — 6

Growing from seeds or cuttings — 8

COMMON VARIETIES OF CULINARY HERBS — 11
- Basil — 11
- Chives — 12
- Coriander — 13
- Dill — 14
- Mint — 15
- Parsley — 17
- Rosemary — 18
- Sage — 18
- Tarragon — 19
- Thyme — 20

COMMON VARIETIES OF MEDICINAL HERBS — 22
- Basil — 23
- Chamomile — 24
- Chives — 25
- Coriander — 26
- Dill — 26
- Echinacea — 27
- Feverfew — 28
- Pansies — 29
- Lavender — 30
- Lemon Balm — 31

Marigold	32
Mint	33
Parsley	34
Rosemary	35
Sage	36
Tarragon	37
Thyme	37

Harvesting, drying, and storage — 39

RECIPES — 42

Fresh basil pesto	42
Roasted Piedmontese peppers	44
Cheese and chive coleslaw	46
Lemon and chive pesto	48
Watermelon, halloumi and herb salad	49
Moroccan herb and almond couscous	51
Dill sauce	53
Dill with broad beans	54
Echinacea tea	56
Spicy chicken with an Asian salad	57
Mint and goji quinoa	59
Parsley tempura	61
Parsley sauce	62
Rosemary baked beans	63
Apple, blackberry and rosemary crumble	65
Sage palmiers	67
Spicy sage and butternut mash	69
Tarragon chicken with asparagus	71
Mushroom and tarragon cream	73
Vegetable soup with thyme and chorizo	75
Warm potato salad with thyme and shallot dressing	77

History and uses of herbs

"What is Paradise? But a Garden, an Orchard of Trees and Herbs, full of pleasure and nothing there but delights."
William Lawson, explorer, 1618

The purpose of this book is to help you cultivate your own little corner of paradise on a balcony, roof terrace or even a windowsill indoors. One of the many delights of herbs is their versatility – they don't necessarily need a garden to become verdant, productive and delicious.

Most people grow herbs for use in cooking – to complement or enhance the flavours of dishes. Think how rosemary and mint enhance lamb, or how dill complements salmon. Fresh herbs taste fresher and stronger than dried herbs, and if you use them straight after picking you'll enjoy not just intensity of flavour, but also higher vitamin content.

For millennia, man has had a fond, sometimes mystical, and often essential, relationship with herbs, for medicinal as well as culinary reasons. Herbs were not only used to flavour and preserve food or disguise the taste of old meat, they were also recognised for their health benefits.

For example, Ayurveda, the holistic Indian healing system that dates back 5,000 years, relies heavily on the use of herbs and spices in medicine and food to balance the body and mind. Between 300BC and 200AD, a book on medicinal plants and agriculture was written in China, based upon knowledge handed down by Emperor Shen Nong (The Divine Farmer) who lived around 2800BC. As well as documenting methods of seed preservation, the book described over 300 plants, listing their medicinal uses and categorising them in terms of strength and toxicity.

At around 1550BC, the Egyptians recorded some 700 plant-based remedies for common medical complaints on a 20-metre scroll of papyrus, now known as Ebers Papyrus. Later, Hippocrates in the first century BC and Galen in the second century AD developed Greek herbal medicine – considered the foundation of modern medicine – for the treatment of ailments. More recently, colonists and settlers in the Northern and Southern hemispheres discovered local herbs and plants that had been used for medicinal purposes by the indigenous populations for aeons. An example is

Echinacea, native to North America, which is still used today for the treatment of common infections.

Today, 80% of botanicals-based pharmaceutical drugs are used to treat the very same conditions identified by herbalists of the past. The healing power of plants has certainly stood the test of time and it's reassuring to think that something so natural forms the basis of modern medicine. And the fact that herbs are so good for you is another great reason to grow them yourself and include them in your cooking.

Getting started

Your first step is to decide which herbs you want to grow and whether you'll be growing them from seeds, young plants or cuttings. Wherever possible, use organic seeds, plants or cuttings from reputable suppliers: many herbs are used raw in dishes and you will want to minimise the pesticides and chemicals you consume.

Different herbs have different requirements for healthy growth, so if you're new to gardening it's best to start out by growing a small selection of herbs that you know you will use, before becoming more adventurous later with the benefit of experience.

Most herbs like to grow in well-drained soil, so the containers you select should have drainage holes at the bottom. Put a few stones or pebbles in the base of the pot and add gravel to the growing medium to further improve drainage. The best type of container for herbs are unglazed clay pots, because they allow soil to dry out in between watering, prevent overly-wet roots and allow for the circulation of air. At first you should aim for a separate pot for each type of herb; later you can get adventurous (and artistic) by combining herbs with the same soil and moisture requirements in the same pot. An example would be a pot of purple sage, brimming with trailing thyme: smells heavenly, looks stunning!

In the same way that we need to eat a healthy diet, plants need to get the right nutrients from soil. The emphasis should be on feeding the soil, rather than the plant – which includes keeping everything as organic as possible. The balance of growing medium will depend upon the herb you're growing and you need to decide if you're going to use a soil mix or a soilless mix.

A **soil mix** uses equal parts of organic compost, topsoil and sand, with organic fertiliser mixed through. A **soilless mix** combines one part perlite, one part vermiculite with four to six parts of peat moss, topped up with nutrients such as lime or oyster shell to achieve the pH appropriate to the herb you're intending to grow.

The amount of watering required also varies from herb to herb, so check on each herb's needs and water accordingly. Herbs won't thrive in soggy conditions, which will cause their roots to rot, so water them sparingly and only when the top layer of growing medium starts to feel dry. If necessary, use a soil moisture metre to help.

Windowsill gardening

Although herbs that are grown inside have slightly less flavour than those grown outside, they are far easier to maintain and monitor. Weeding is not required and garden pests are kept at bay, plus there's the additional advantage of fresh herbs all year long.

Decide on the best place to grow your herbs. A windowsill, preferably south- or west-facing, is the perfect spot to grow herbs indoors because they need plenty of sunshine. In winter months, you might struggle to ensure that your herbs get the hours of sunlight they need each day, so supplement winter sunshine with grow lights to keep your herbs healthy.

Balcony or roof terrace gardening

Herbs grown on balconies or roof terraces not only look lovely, they smell fabulous too when you're sitting nearby. Although they require more work and attention than windowsill herbs, they more than compensate with abundant growth and stronger flavours.

The location of your outdoor herb garden will also be determined sunshine, bearing in mind that herbs require six to eight hours of sunshine a day. For this reason you should avoid placing your herbs in overly shady corners, as well as exposed areas where intense sunshine or strong winds could harm them.

Plants in pots dry out more quickly than those embedded in soil, so potted outside herbs will require regular monitoring and watering – morning and evening in the summer. Ensure that you bring your potted herbs inside before the first frosts arrive, placing them in a suitably sunny indoor location, such as on a windowsill.

Growing from seeds or cuttings

Most herbs can be planted from seeds, but some herbs grow better from cuttings. Examples are mint, oregano, rosemary and French tarragon.

If **growing herbs from seed**, assemble your pots and growing medium as outlined above. To begin with, plant the seeds for each different herb in a separate pot according to the instructions on the corresponding seed packet, before watering well. To encourage the seeds to germinate and retain moisture, put each pot in a plastic bag or cover the top of it with cling film, then place it on a sunny windowsill or in another warm spot with an ambient temperature of between 15C and 23C. Check the pot(s) regularly to ensure the soil is still moist, lightly water/mist as required, then – as soon as the first seedling appears – remove the plastic wrapping. Move each pot to a sunny position and water them regularly, according to the needs of the herb they contain.

Growing herbs from cuttings can prove equally rewarding. First of all, you need to select the right area of stem from a mature plant to use as a cutting. It's easiest to grow cuttings from softwood stems (many of which require only water to produce roots), which you can take from a plant in spring or early summer while it is still growing. You can tell a softwood cutting from its pliable, green lower section. You can also grow cuttings from semi-hardwood stems, which are also pliable but brown in colour. Note that semi-hardwood cuttings tend to take better in soil or sand than in water. Attempting to use hardwood stems (the previous year's dry, woody growth) to grow cuttings is not recommended.

Take several cuttings, ideally around 20cm long, from the plant that you want to grow. Cut each cutting just below the leaf node then gently pinch off the leaves at the two leaf nodes above the cut. Depending upon whether your cuttings are softwood or semi-hardwood, place them in either water or a soil-sand mixture, and wrap the pot and cuttings in a plastic bag to encourage humidity. After three to four weeks your cuttings should have grown a tumble of healthy roots, at which point you can move them into permanent pots filled with an appropriate growing medium.

Once your seedlings have grown into young plants, you might want to consider **pinching, or topping**, them. This involves the removal of an upper portion of stem to encourage leaf growth below, resulting in a shorter, bushier and leafier plant – and more herbs for your kitchen! Where a leaf meets the stem you will see a small knob, which is in fact a dormant leaf bud. This won't grow while there is growth above it, but if you pinch off the stem above the bud it will realise it needs to start growing. Dormant leaf buds tend to grow in pairs, so if you remove the stem above, both leaf buds will grow to produce two new stems, where only one grew before. Quite quickly, you will notice that your herb has become thicker and more productive.

Common Varieties of Culinary Herbs

Basil

Basil, originally native to Asia and India where it is known as *tulsi*, has been cultivated there for more than 5,000 years. There are many different types of basil – purple basil, Thai basil, lemon basil – but the one found most frequently in British kitchens is the bright green Genovese basil. Its name derives from the Greek word for 'royal' – *basileus* – allegedly because basil was growing at the site in Jerusalem where St Helena found the true cross.

Provided you give it enough sunlight (at least four hours of full sun a day), basil is a rewarding herb to grow because it's exuberant, hardy and relatively free of pests and diseases. If you're struggling for sunshine in the winter, the good news is that basil does equally well under fluorescent bulbs held 5-10cm away from the leaves.

Basil likes temperatures of around 20C and a moist growing medium. Mist the plant regularly and use weak liquid fertiliser on a weekly basis. Basil grows well from seed and the warmer the temperature, the quicker the germination time. Once your basil has some robust leafy stems, start topping the main stalk to encourage it to grow outwards, rather than upwards. You might see flowers forming about 75 days after planting, so snip them off quickly to prolong the vegetable phase. You can still eat basil after it has flowered, but it is likely to taste bitter.

Chives

Related to onion and garlic, chives are hardy perennials that are native to Europe and Asia. Different varieties of wild chive are found in different parts of the world, but the one that is most commonly cultivated today is closest to a variety that originates in the Alps. The two types of chive most often encountered are the common chive (which feature pinky-purple pompom flowers in the spring) and the garlic (or Chinese) chive, which produces white, star-shaped blooms in the summer. As the name suggests, the garlic chive has a garlicky taste and smell.

Chives thrive best in at least six hours of full sun each day. Turn your chive plant around regularly to encourage upright growth, because the leaves tend to bend towards the sun. You can top up your chive plant's sunlight quota using indoor plant lights for 14 hours a day, held 15cm away from the plant. Like basil, chives like moist but well-drained soil and a warm room of around 16–24C. Use herb fertiliser in the soil during spring, summer and autumn.

Coriander

The strong fragrance of coriander leaves, which reminded the Greeks of the smell of insects (*koros* means insect, while *koriannon* means bug), gave rise to the name of this herb. Coriander is also known by its Spanish name *cilantro*, which also derives from Greek. A relative of parsley, coriander is used for both its seeds and its leaves.

Coriander has a rich history: its seeds have been found in the tombs of ancient Egyptians; the Greeks, Chinese and Egyptians lauded it for its aphrodisiac properties; it is referred to in Sanskrit writings and the Bible; it was one of the first herbs grown by American colonists. Interestingly, it is one of the few herbs used in the Chinese kitchen.

A wonderful addition many dishes (in particular Thai and Indian cuisine), coriander can be tricky to grow because of its tendency to flower quickly. To avoid early flowering, try the 'calypso' variety if you are growing coriander for its leaves, as opposed to its seeds (where flowers are obviously crucial to seed production). Keep picking mature leaves as and when you need them, as this will also help to delay flowering.

Coriander will thrive indoors on a bright windowsill that avoids direct sunlight (it needs four to five hours of sun a day). It's a delicate plant that likes to live in moist, but never wet, soil. You can top up with a growing light if your plant is not getting enough sunshine. To encourage a bushier plant, pinch out the growing tips.

Dill

As its appearance and taste suggest, dill is related to the fennel plant. Its name has Norse origins and means 'to lull or soothe', in recognition of its stomach-calming and sleep-inducing properties.

Dill has been significant throughout history. It is mentioned in the Ebers Papyrus and was found extensively in the gardens of Greeks and Romans, who wove it into victory crowns for athletes and war heroes, or used its pretty fronds to provide fragrance and decoration during banquets. In the Bible, dill is mentioned as an herb that was tithed. Later, during the Middle Ages, dill was used to protect against witchcraft and evil spirits.

Like many Mediterranean herbs, dill enjoys sunlight, requiring six to eight hours a day. In winter months you may need to use grow lights 12 hours a day, held 20cm away from these delicate plants. Dill needs regular (not over-) watering, but only add water once the soil appears dry. Adding diluted liquid fertiliser or fish fertiliser to the growing medium every six weeks is recommended.

Dill is a tall plant and can grow up to 90cm – not ideal for indoor gardening! – so use stakes to contain growth and keep the plant upright. You might also want to consider buying a dwarf variety, such as 'Fernleaf', or one developed for container gardens, such as 'Ella'.

Mint

Mint is a wonderfully versatile herb, which can be used in so many different ways. From iced tea to garnish, from ice cream to couscous, there's a place for mint in a wide variety of dishes.

Mint's name originates from an enchanting piece of Greek mythology. Hades (God of the Underworld) fell in love with a beautiful young water nymph named Minthe. When Hades' wife, Persephone, discovered this, she was enraged and – in a fit of jealousy – turned Minthe into a lowly plant that would be trodden on underfoot. Pluto tried to undo Persephone's curse, to no avail. He could only ensure that the plant would produce a sweet smell when stepped upon. Over time, the name Minthe became Mentha and, later, regional variations such as *menthe* (French) and mint.

Mint grows enthusiastically but its roots (runners) are invasive, producing new plants and leaves as they go. This is good news for indoor gardeners because the result is a fast-growing plant that is best grown in a pot or other container. Use regular potting compost or an equal combination or sand, peat, and perlite. Locate your pot of mint in a spot that enjoys sun early in the morning and partial afternoon shade. Mint needs regular watering: it's vital to not let the soil in its pot dry out.

Pick sprigs of mint often to postpone flowering and pinch off the flower buds when they appear. Mist your mint plant and rotate it regularly so that the plant takes on an even shape. Mint will enjoy an occasional dose of diluted liquid fertiliser, but take care not to add too much or you'll impact the herb's flavour.

Parsley

Parsley, a relative of celery, originates from the Mediterranean. For an herb that's bursting with antioxidants and other important nutrients, it's strange to think that parsley was associated with death by so many of our forefathers. This is possibly because of its close resemblance to fool's parsley, a toxic plant. Parsley exists in curly and flat leaf form and, aside from appearance, there is little to differentiate them as they both taste similar and contain roughly the same amount of nutrients. Be careful to wash curly parsley carefully, because grit and soil tends to cling to the leaves.

Parsley grows best if it receives six to eight hours of direct sunlight daily, which you can top up in winter months with plant lights. Parsley enjoys regularly misting, although this won't be necessary if you're growing it in a humid room like the kitchen. Keep the soil nicely moist and turn the plant regularly to ensure it grows evenly and upright. Water parsley regularly, draining the saucer beneath the pot after watering to prevent waterlogging the toots, and feed it every two weeks with diluted liquid fertiliser.

Rosemary

Easy, hardy, evergreen rosemary is a delightfully robust herb to cultivate, and has many uses in the kitchen all year round. The Greeks and Romans appreciated the healing power of rosemary and used it to assist the memory: students would braid it into their hair or wear it in garlands around their necks during exams. Later, the Romans introduced rosemary to Britain, where it was feted as a cosmetic, a cure for gout and an elixir of youth.

This bushy perennial originates from the Mediterranean, and its name comes about from the Latin for 'dew of the sea' – *ros* (dew) and *marinus* (sea). It grows best in warm, dry conditions, so place your pot of rosemary in a warm, sunny place and water it sparingly in soil that drains well, because waterlogged soil can rot its roots and kill the plant. Add lime to your growing medium because alkaline soil increases rosemary's fragrance.

Sage

Sage derives its name from *suage* (Old French), which is itself derived from the Latin word *salvia*, from *salvus*, meaning 'healthy'. This speaks of the many healing properties of sage, which was used by the ancient

Egyptians to treat infertility, by the Greeks for wounds, sores and coughs, and extensively since.

Another Mediterranean herb, sage now grows happily in many parts of the world. Sage likes a lot of light, so place your pot of sage on a sunny windowsill and try to ensure it receives six to eight hours of full sun each day in temperatures of around 20C. Supplement sunlight with plant lights if your plant's growth seems sluggish, keeping the light around 20cm away from the leaves. Sage likes humidity, so mist it periodically, and make sure its soil is only slightly moist.

Tarragon

Related (perhaps surprisingly) to the sunflower, this small, shrubby herb is native to Southern Russia and Western Asia. Tarragon's name derives from *dracunculus*, Latin for 'a little dragon', on account of the shape of its roots, which resemble a curling dragon's tail.

Two main types of tarragon are cultivated today. French tarragon has the tang of aniseed and is sweet and aromatic. Russian tarragon, possessing coarse, pale leaves, is slightly bitter and not fragrant. Understandably, the French tarragon is more often used in cooking.

Tarragon likes bright light (preferably six to eight hours a day), dry soil, and temperatures around 20C. Be careful not to overwater the plant, allowing the top layer of soil to dry out before watering again, and mist it every couple of days. Add a light dilution of liquid or fish fertiliser every couple of weeks.

Thyme

The origins of the name thyme are – if you'll excuse the pun – a bit misty, but it's generally agreed that it comes from the Latin *fumus* or Greek *thumos*, both meaning 'smoke'. The name possibly refers to the fact that thyme was used in temples and churches during sacrificial ceremonies, or to the clouds of fragrance unleashed by the herb when you crush it.

Thyme does best in temperatures of 15C or higher with around six hours of daylight. Although it prefers sunny locations, thyme also tolerates indirect light. Water your thyme plant regularly, but only after the top layer of soil has dried out, to avoid water logging the roots. Every fortnight, feed the soil with a diluted liquid or fish fertilizer. If the stems on your thyme plant are starting to look woody, cut them back to encourage new growth. Remove flowers to encourage leaf production, which you could dry for later use in tea.

If roots start growing out of the bottom of your thyme pot, you will need to transplant the thyme to a larger container. Thyme plants can be divided easily, leading to even more plants, either to grow for yourself or to give away as gifts.

Common Varieties of Medicinal Herbs

"The garden is the poor man's apothecary."
– German proverb

Even before herbs were used in cooking, they were recognised by our forefathers for their medicinal uses. As noted earlier, herbal extracts are used extensively in modern medicine, indicating that our ancestors were onto something when they noticed their healing properties all those years ago.

There is often an interesting correlation between poisonous plants and those that are used in modern-day medicine. For example, the common foxglove has extremely poisonous leaves, consumption of which could lead to severe headaches, vomiting, and even death. However, extracts from these leaves are used in medicine to control the heart rate. Likewise, the leaves and berries of deadly nightshade are extremely poisonous, but one of their constituents – atropine – is used to treat heart attacks. An extract of it was also used as a beauty product in times gone by – to make a woman's pupils dilate. Poison hemlock can cause respiratory collapse, but is used today to arrest spasms or as a sedative.

Luckily, herbs are not poisonous, and their presence in our food is almost always beneficial.

Basil

Basil is a natural anti-inflammatory, containing similar compounds to oregano and medical marijuana – without inducing a consequent high. Its anti-inflammatory properties can help to combat irritable bowel, flatulence, and rheumatoid arthritis.

Basil is high in antioxidants, especially in its oil or extracts forms, which help to prevent the free radical damage associated with cancer, ageing and skin conditions. Regular doses of basil extract and oils are considered a supremely safe way of ingesting these beneficial compounds, as well as boosting your immune system.

The antibacterial properties of fresh basil leaves and oil make them suitable for application to wounds in order to eliminate infections. They can also be used as disinfectants on work surfaces. If used frequently in cooking, basil can help combat common viruses, such as herpes, colds and flu.

Basil contains cinnamanic acid, which can improve breathing, stabilise blood sugar and enhance circulation. Accordingly, naturopathic doctors often prescribe it to treat allergies, respiratory disorders, diabetes, infertility and impotence.

Chamomile

This pretty daisy-like herb has been used medicinally for centuries to relieve digestive disorders, wounds, skin inflammations and stress, thanks to its anti-inflammatory, antioxidant and antimicrobial properties. There are also indications that chamomile can help sufferers of diabetes and hyperglycaemia, as well as muscle spasms and menstrual cramps. Chamomile's stress-relieving properties mean that it also helps to promote sleep.

Chamomile is best ingested as an infusion or a tea, with German chamomile being the best variety for this purpose. Harvest entire chamomile flowers head as soon as they bloom (for the best flavoured tea) and dry them to make tea. Harvesting the flowers in this way will help to promote more growth.

Chamomile grows happily in containers on a balcony or a windowsill, preferring full sun to partial shade and moist, but not soggy, soil. You can propagate those using seeds, which should germinate within two weeks of planting, or cuttings, using 7-12cm of stem tips. The plants don't need much supplemental fertiliser and are fairly pest-resistant, although do look out for aphids.

Chives

Chives are rich in flavonoids, and therefore possess not only anti-inflammatory effects but also anti-cancer properties. Research has shown that chives can help to reduce the effects of rheumatoid arthritis, as well as reduce the incidence of prostate and gastrointestinal tract cancers. Chives can also help to reduce blood pressure and hypertension, improve eyesight and promote healthy skin.

Rich in vitamins C and E and multiple minerals, chives contain abundant nutrients and have antioxidant properties that reduce cell damage from free radicals, helping to prevent cancer, heart problems and degenerative ailments, while boosting the metabolism and promoting healthy tissue. Use chives liberally in your cooking to enjoy all of their health benefits.

Coriander

Coriander's deep green leaves are rich in antioxidants, vitamins, minerals, essential oils, and dietary fibre. Many of its vitamin (vitamin A, beta carotene, vitamin C, folic acid, niacin and riboflavin) and mineral (potassium, calcium, manganese, iron and magnesium) constituents are vital for optimal health. A 100g portion of coriander provides 30%, 225% and 258% of an individual's recommended daily intake of vitamin C, vitamin A and vitamin K, respectively. This makes it extremely important for boosting the immune system, promoting healthy skin and eyes, strengthening bones and helping to prevent Alzheimer's disease.

Dill

This feathery herb appears to offer multiple health benefits. Dill, like coriander, contains significant amounts of antioxidants, vitamin A and vitamin C and trace amounts of iron, manganese and folic acid. The essential oils it contains stimulate the digestive tract, easing constipation, excess gas and hiccups. Dill's essential oils contain flavonoids and vitamin B complex, which stimulate the secretion of enzymes and hormones that produce a calming and hypnotic effect, to assist with a good night's sleep.

Dill possesses antimicrobial and anti-fungal properties, which mean it can help to combat infections caused by microbes (such as diarrhoea and skin infections) or fungus (such as dysentery and skin conditions), and for this reason it is also good for oral hygiene, having been used in the past to clean teeth and freshen breath. Dill's high calcium content can protect against osteoporosis and assist with bone repair, while its anti-inflammatory properties have long been used to help combat arthritis and gout.

Certain components of dill's essential oils help to ease congestion in the respiratory tract, where this is caused by allergies, coughs or histamine. They also help to stimulate the secretion of hormones that promote a healthy menstrual cycle. Finally, the abundance of antioxidants found in dill can help in the prevention of cancer.

Echinacea

Echinacea is an extract from the Eastern Purple Coneflower, a member of the daisy family, which is a North American plant that has been used for centuries as an herbal remedy for the common cold. A recent clinical study found that regular consumption of Echinacea reduced the number of colds acquired by frequent cold sufferers and the duration of each illness by an average of 26%. It seems that

Echinacea stimulates phagocytosis (the consumption by lymphocytes and white blood cells of invading organisms) by 20-40%, and also inhibits the ability of bacteria to gain access to healthy cells. It is also being increasingly used for external treatments, as it slows down bacterial growth, kills bacteria, and combats inflammation.

Echinacea is a large plant, so only suitable for growing indoors if you have enough space. It would, however, make a bold and attractive addition to a balcony or terrace garden. Find a generous pot, fill it with well-watered (but not soggy) growing medium, scatter Echinacea seeds over the top, and then cover with a further light layer of soil, before lightly watering. Place the pot in a well-lit spot and expect the seeds to germinate within 10-20 days. Keep the plant regularly watered. If you plant early enough, you can expect flowers within the first year.

Feverfew

Often confused with chamomile on account of its appearance, Feverfew is a native of the Balkan Mountains. It contains a compound called parthenolide, which helps to inhibit the inflammation that can lead to migraines, provided the Feverfew extract is of high quality and consumed at the onset of the headache. For centuries,

Feverfew has been used to reduce the pain and inflammation associated with arthritis. It is also thought to inhibit the growth of cancer cells and can be used as an insect repellent.

Feverfew needs sunshine to flourish and is best suited to a sunny, outdoor spot on a terrace or balcony, rather than indoors, where the plants can get leggy.

Pansies

Pansies, also known as a violet, johnny-jump-up or heartsease (and more formally as the Viola tricolor), is a vibrant and enchanting annual, the leaves and flowers of which are both edible. Pansy leaves are crunchy and can be used as an entire substitute for lettuce, and their lovely flowers will enhance the taste and look of any dish.

Pansies contain salicylic acid, which is a pain reliever, and were historically used to treat headaches and sore throats. They are also anti-fungal, antiseptic, and anti-inflammatory, with expectorant and diuretic qualities, hence their use as a breath-freshener and in countering whooping cough, cystitis, eczema, acne, psoriasis, cradle cap and rheumatic complaints.

Easy to grow, both indoors and outdoors, pansies can be grown from seed or from seedlings bought in a garden centre. Sow them in early spring in rich organic soil that drains well, cover them with 3mm of soil, water them regularly and keep them warm. They do best in a sunny position but are constantly thirsty, so water them well and regularly. With proper attention, and regular dead heading, pansies will bloom from spring through autumn, and self-seed in the process, so you will see new plants every year.

Lavender

People place lavender in pillows for a reason: for centuries it has been used to induce calm, relaxation and sleep, and today lavender oil is still used to treat insomnia, depression, anxiety and restlessness. Lavender also has anti-inflammatory and antiseptic properties (its name comes from the Latin word *lavare*, meaning 'to wash), and can be used to treat minor cuts, burns and insect bites.

French lavender (which has pretty serrated leaves) is the best variety of lavender to grow indoors. Lavender loves sun, so you'll need to find a really sunny spot for it that will give it at least eight hours of sunlight a day, or supplement sunlight with grow lights. As a Mediterranean plant, lavender likes to grow in hot and dry conditions. Water regularly, but only once the soil feels dry to the touch, as lavender hates nothing more than soggy roots – these lead to health problems.

As your lavender plant grows, it may need re-potting, but do bear in mind that it likes to have snug roots in well-drained spaces, so you'll need to choose your pot accordingly. Lavender can be pruned in the spring or autumn to maintain the appearance and shape of the plant. Cut back un-shapely stalks, saving them for drying later, and ensure that green growth remains after you've pruned. The plant might look a little shocked at first, but new growth should appear quite quickly.

Lemon Balm

A member of the mint family, lemon balm has been used for generations to counter anxiety, induce sleep and relieve indigestion. The ancient Greeks and Romans used lemon balm as an insect repellent (its oils contain citronella and other compounds that repel bugs) and to treat insect bites and stings.

Lemon balm is rich in anti-oxidants and possesses antibacterial and antiviral properties, which make it effective in treating eczema, herpes, mumps and throat infections. Crush two to four tablespoons of crushed lemon balm leaves and add to a cup of boiling water.

Lemon balm does well as a houseplant, provided it receives at least six hours of sunlight a day, or the equivalent using supplemental light from grow lamps. Make sure your plant is regularly watered, but avoid water logging it, and cut it back regularly (use the leaves in salads or to garnish desserts) to maintain its shape.

Marigold

Marigold, native to the Mediterranean, has gained popularity throughout the world over the centuries. The ancient Egyptians believed it had rejuvenating powers, while the Greeks used it in cooking. Gods and goddesses were adorned with marigolds (and marigolds are still used as offerings to this day) in India and, during the Middle Ages, young girls drank potions containing marigolds in an attempt to discover who they might marry.

Marigold has anti-inflammatory properties, which make it suitable for the treatment of burns, bruising, skin conditions and certain allergies. They contain abundant quantities of antioxidants, which can lessen the effects of free radicals and protect the eyes from cataracts, and lycopene – a compound that lowers the risk of prostate cancer and heart disease. The flowers and leaves of marigolds are known to be effective against breast, melanoma, colon and leukaemia cancers, as well as mouth and stomach ulcers. On a cosmetic level, marigold can help to balance an oily complexion, and eliminate scabies and warts.

Marigolds grow well indoors, but it's best to choose a dwarf variety that will look compact on your windowsill. You can grow marigolds using seedlings from garden centres, or from seed. If growing from seed, fill a pot three quarters full with potting compost; scatter the marigold seeds over the top, then over with a further 3mm layer of compost, watering well. Cover the pot with plastic and allow the seeds to germinate on a light windowsill; this will take up to 14 days, depending upon the ambient temperature. Once the seedlings are showing two leaves, remove the plastic, spray lightly with water if the soil is dry, and continue to monitor the plants. Deadhead the flowers regularly to encourage more blooms.

Mint

Mint would appear to alleviate a whole raft of health complaints, making it a very valuable addition to both your herb garden and your kitchen.

Mint's aroma stimulates the salivary glands, which in turn prompt the production of digestive enzymes, facilitating digestion. This is why mint is often used to relieve motion sickness and nausea. Mint balms or oils rubbed on the forehead and around the nose can alleviate headaches, thanks to mint's anti-inflammatory qualities.

Mint's piercing aroma also helps to clear nasal, throat, lung and bronchial congestion, as well as soothing the throat. The aromas of mint help to alleviate depression, anxiety and fatigue: a few drops of mint essential oil on your pillow at night can work wonders. Mint's stimulating qualities also have a positive effect on memory and alertness, while its antiseptic properties make it an excellent skin cleanser and contributor to oral health.

Parsley

Parsley is more than just decoration on your plate: it's packed with so many nutrients and antioxidants that it's almost a meal in itself. It contains high levels of vitamins A, C, B12 and K, all of which help to boost the immune system, counter inflammation, suppress the development of cancers and help the nervous system.

The folic acid in parsley contributes towards a healthy heart, circulatory system and blood pressure. This combination of vitamins can help to arrest the development of cancers. Parsley not only encourages digestions, it also cleanses the palate and freshens the breath, making it the perfect *digestif* at the end of a meal!

Rosemary

In the past, rosemary was used more frequently as a medicine than in the kitchen because our forefathers believed it could cure nightmares, madness, anxiety and impotence. It was also used when dressing the bodies of the deceased, possibly to counter the smell of decay.

The oils in rosemary have anti-inflammatory, antiseptic, anti-allergic and anti-fungal properties, making it suitable for fighting infections. Its leaves contain high levels of vitamins A, B-complex (folic acid) and C, as well as the minerals calcium, copper, iron, magnesium, manganese and potassium.

As well as helping memory and concentration, rosemary can improve your mood (inhaling the aroma of lavender causes cortisol levels to drop) and freshen your breath.

Sage

As suggested by the origins of its name (salvia means 'to heal'), sage has been used as a medicinal herb for centuries. John Gerard, the herbalist (1545-1611), gave this account of the perceived benefits of the herb: *"Sage is singularly good for the head and brain, it quickeneth the senses and memory, strengtheneth the sinews, restoreth health to those that have the palsy, and taketh away shaky trembling of the members."*

These early observations have been supported by recent research that identified improvements in memory and cognitive function in patients who were prescribed regular doses of sage extract. It is believed that sage inhibits the loss of acetylcholine, a chemical messenger in the brain – a discovery that could be of particular benefit to Alzheimer's sufferers.

Sage contains antibacterial, antiseptic and antifungal properties, making it effective in fighting bacteria, such as E. coli, and fungal infections. For these reasons, it can make an effective mouthwash, providing relief for throat and mount infections.

Tarragon

High in vitamins, minerals and antioxidants, tarragon provides several benefits to health. The ancient Greeks used it as a cure for toothache because of its ability to numb the mouth and, indeed, research has shown that tarragon contains high levels of eugenol, a pain-relieving agent. Tarragon encourages the liver to produce bile and so assists with digestion; it can also stimulate the appetite in the old and infirm. It can help to relieve stress, anxiety, and insomnia, as well as promoting good heart health due to chemicals that keep the blood vessels clean.

Thanks to its high levels of potassium and beta-carotene, tarragon is good for eye health and function, as well as supporting female reproductive health. Recent research has found that Russian tarragon can enhance muscle mass by increasing the absorption of muscle creatine.

Thyme

Thyme contains the active ingredient thymol, which is a strong antiseptic and antifungal agent. For this reason, thyme oil can be used for many different purposes, from the treatment of acne and other skin conditions, to arresting fungal infections and preserving food.

Research has also found that thymol, in combination with other compounds, can kill off Tiger mosquito larvae, the adults of which carry dengue fever, chikungunya, yellow fever, West Nile virus and St Louis encephalitis. There is also evidence to indicate that wild thyme can reduce hypertension, and help in arresting cell division in breast- and colon-cancer cells.

Harvesting, drying, and storage

The optimal time for harvesting herbs is when their flavour and aroma are at their peak. This will vary according to the type of herb you are growing, which part of the plant you are using and what you are intending to use it for.

If you are using the leaves of an herb, their flavour is better before the herb flowers, so harvest the leaves before flowering (preferably in the morning), but leave behind enough leaves to maintain the plant's growth. Harvesting before flowering also helps to stop the number of leaves declining.

An herb's flowers (such as chamomile) have the strongest concentration of oil and flavour just before the flower bud opens. Tarragon or lavender flowers can be harvested in early summer, before shearing the plants to half their height in order to encourage a second flowering in the early autumn.

Herb roots should be harvested in the autumn after the leaves have faded. If you are growing an herb for its seeds, harvest them as the seedpods change from green to brown or grey in colour, but before the pods burst open.

Although herbs contain more nutrients and flavours when eaten fresh, they still add flavour to dishes when preserved in dried form. Some herbs (such as sage, thyme, dill and parsley) dry easily, while others (mint, basil or tarragon) can go mouldy or discolour if they're not dried quickly.

To maximise flavours, harvest the herbs in the morning, just before they flower. Rinse off dust or dirt from the leaves using cold water (don't do this if the plant is clean), shake the excess water away, then spread out the herbs to dry on clean kitchen paper until the surface moisture has evaporated, removing any dead or damaged foliage in the process. Once dry on the outside, gather the stems into small bunches, tie them with string, then hang them upside down in a dark, dry spot, with good air circulation.

While less traditional, it's in fact quicker and easier to dry herbs in the microwave or a conventional oven. Put a piece of kitchen roll in the microwave, scatter a single layer of dry, clean leaves over it, place another piece of kitchen roll on top, then microwave on high for one to two minutes. Let the leaves cool down, see if they are brittle and, if they're not, repeat the process for 30 seconds at a time until they are. If your herbs have thick leaves, start out by air-drying them for a few days in advance.

If you're drying your herbs using a conventional oven, preheat it to 80C, place the seeds or leaves in a thin layer on a flat baking sheet and put them in the oven for between two and four hours.

Once herbs are brittle and crumbly, they are sufficiently dried for storage. Separate the leaves from their stems and store them whole (to maximise flavour, only crush them when you're about to use them) in airtight glass or plastic jars. During the first few days, examine the stored herbs to ensure that no mould or moisture is forming; if it is, you'll need to repeat the drying process. The herbs will keep for around a year if the jars are stored in a cool, dry place. If you're drying seeds, store them whole to preserve their flavour and grind them when required.

Another way to preserve herbs is to freeze them. Basil, chives and dill can be frozen straight after washing, while other herbs require blanching first. Wash the herbs well, and then dunk them in boiling water for 50 seconds, before plunging them into iced water, packaging them and freezing them. Alternatively, washed herbs can be roughly chopped, then added in generous pinches to ice cube trays half-filled with water before freezing. Pop out the herby ice cubes into bags and use in cooking as required.

Recipes

All the recipes listed below will feed four people, unless otherwise stated.

Fresh basil pesto

Few recipes capture the vibrant, fresh flavours of basil as well as this classic pesto. As well as being a real crowd-pleaser, it's quick and easy to make, too.

Ingredients:

50g pine nuts (or cashew nuts)

A large bunch of basil

50g parmesan (or pecorino)

150ml olive oil

2 cloves of garlic

Method:

Roast the pine nuts briefly until golden brown, either in the oven or in a dry frying pan over a moderate heat. Add to a food processor, along with the other ingredients, and blitz until smooth, adding salt and pepper to taste.

You can use the pesto straight away, or store it in the fridge for up to two weeks by pouring it into a jar, then pouring a light layer of oil on top to stop it from turning dark.

Tip: you can swap unsalted cashew nuts for pine nuts and pecorino for parmesan, giving similar results that are easier on the wallet!

Roasted Piedmontese peppers

A tasty, flexible and easy starter for any dinner party, or a light supper for two.

Ingredients:

8 or 12 ripe tomatoes

4 large red peppers, halved through the stalk (leaving the stalk on) and deseeded

4 garlic cloves, finely sliced

5-6 tbsp olive oil

8 large anchovies from a can, halved lengthways

A small handful of fresh basil

Method:

Preheat your oven to 190C or gas mark 5. Put the tomatoes in a bowl then pour boiling water over them, leaving them for a few minutes. Fish them out one at a time with a slotted spoon and peel off their skins. Place the peppers, cut side facing upwards, on a baking tray, tuck a few pieces of garlic inside each one, followed by 2 or 3 tomatoes (depending upon the size of the tomatoes and the room available). Sprinkle with salt and pepper, spoon over the olive oil and bake in the oven for around 45 minutes, being careful not to let them burn. Remove from the oven, transfer the peppers to plates, drape two anchovy halves over each pepper half in an x-formation, drizzle with the juices from the tray and scatter basil leaves over each pepper half.

Tip: vegetarians can enjoy this dish too, if you omit the anchovies and beef up the salt.

Cheese and chive coleslaw

A fresh and nutritious accompaniment to picnics and barbeques.

Ingredients:

400g white cabbage, finely sliced

1 carrot, grated coarsely

1 red onion, finely sliced

3 tbsp mayonnaise

3 tbsp natural yoghurt

1 tsp mustard

20g chives

100g grated cheddar (or similar cheese)

Method:

Combine all the ingredients (apart from the cheese) in a large bowl, reserving a few chives, and season to taste.

Cover, then chill in the fridge. Before serving, scatter the coleslaw with the cheese and remaining chives.

Lemon and chive pesto

Delicious served with pasta, gnocchi or smeared on crostini.

Ingredients:

1 garlic clove, crushed

Small bunch of chives, finely snipped

Small bunch of parsley, chopped small

2 tbsp pine nuts

2 tbsp parmesan

4 tbsp extra virgin olive oil

Juice and zest of one lemon

Method:

Toast the pine nuts in a dry pan, under a grill or in the oven until golden brown, then chop them finely. Grate the cheese and mix it into the olive oil with the pine nuts, garlic, lemon, chives and parsley.

Watermelon, halloumi and herb salad

A delicious, fresh salad that conjures up the flavours of a summer in Greece.

Ingredients:

1kg of watermelon, chopped into bite-sized cubes and lightly de-seeded

1 small bunch of coriander

1 small bunch of flat-leaf parsley

1 small bunch of mint

240g pack of halloumi cheese cut into bite-sized pieces

Juice and zest of one lemon

4 tbsp olive oil

Method:

Put the melon in a bowl and add the herbs (leaves only). Griddle the halloumi pieces until lightly browned on all sides. Add to the watermelon and herbs once cooled. Whisk together the olive oil, the lemon juice and zest, then pour over the salad. Serve immediately.

Tip: this recipe also tastes great with feta in place of halloumi.

Moroccan herb and almond couscous

A flexible side dish, bursting with North African flavours.

Ingredients:

1 red onion

A pinch of saffron (if you have it)

425ml chicken stock (hot)

1 red chilli

500g couscous

A generous bunch of coriander

50g unsalted, toasted almonds

A handful of dates

The juice of half a lemon

Method:

Cut the onion into slices and fry it in a generous pan until softened, before adding the chilli and cooking for a further minute. Make the stock, adding the saffron strands if you have them, then add the couscous and the stock to the pan. Cover the pan with cling film and leave it for 10 minutes, or until the couscous has absorbed the stock. Chop the dates roughly, strip the coriander leaves from the stalks and stir them, plus the almonds, through the couscous. Add the lemon juice and serve immediately.

Tip: if you're planning to serve this dish cold, omit the coriander from this last step and add it just before serving.

Dill sauce

Dill makes a wonderful accompaniment to fish, and this easy dill sauce will brighten up many fish dishes.

Ingredients:

15g sugar

200ml red wine vinegar

80g Dijon mustard

2 generous tablespoons of chopped, fresh dill

Method:

Whisk together the sugar, vinegar and mustard, then add the oil slowly, whisking as you do so. Once the sauce is smooth and thickened, add the dill and seasoning to taste.

Dill with broad beans

A tasty side dish to accompany fish, best attempted hen broad beans are young and in season.

Ingredients:

450g broad beans in their pods

50ml olive oil

2 onions, finely chopped

2 cloves of garlic, crushed

Juice of half a lemon

250ml vegetable stock

2 tbsp fresh dill, chopped finely

A generous spoonful of Greek yoghurt

Method:

Pop the beans out of their pods and set them to one side. Heat the oil in a large pan and cook the onions and garlic for 2-3 minutes to soften, before adding the beans and lemon juice, stirring to combine. Add the stock, bring to the boil and cook for 15-20 minutes until the beans feel tender. Add the dill and, just before serving, the yoghurt (optional).

Echinacea tea

At the first sign of a cold or flu, mix one part Echinacea (flowers, roots and/or leaves) with a quarter part of lemon grass, a quarter part of mint leaves and some stevia leaves, according to taste. Brew these in boiling water and drink when cooled down.

<u>Spicy chicken with an Asian salad</u>

This light and tasty Asian dish just sings with fresh flavours.

Ingredients:

3 garlic cloves, crushed

2 large red chillies, deseeded and chopped

2 tsp sugar

3 tbsp fish sauce

8 chicken thighs, without skin or bones

2 tbsp vegetable oil

Freshly ground pepper

3 tbsp caster sugar

3 tbsp lime juice

200g fine rice noodles

A handful of fresh mint leaves

2 cucumbers, halved and thinly sliced

4 spring onions, finely sliced

2 tbsp crushed cashew nuts

Method:

Whisk together the garlic, chillies, sugar, fish sauce and peppers to make a marinade. Pour half of the marinade over the chicken and refrigerate for half an hour.

To make the salad dressing, mix the reserved marinade with the sugar and lime juice until the sugar dissolves. Cover the rice noodles with boiling water and set to one side until they have softened, before rinsing them under cold water and draining them. In a large bowl, mix the noodles with the mint, cucumber, spring onions, dressing and crushed cashews.

Shake off the excess marinade from the chicken thighs and fry them on each side in batches in vegetable oil, until they are cooked through. To serve, either divide the salad and chicken among four plates and top with equal portions of chicken, or cut up the chicken into bite-sized pieces and toss through the salad.

Mint and goji quinoa

Vegan, gluten free and packed with superfoods.

Ingredients:

350g quinoa

400g tomatoes

300g fresh parsley

60g fresh mint leaves

4 spring onions

8 tbsp olive oil (extra virgin if possible)

4 tbsp lemon juice

1 garlic clove

1 tsp honey

A handful of goji berries

Salt and pepper

Method:

In a large bowl, cover the quinoa with 700ml of cold water, stir in some salt and soak for at least 8 hours. Drain and rinse the quinoa, then put it in a saucepan, cover it with water and bring to the boil for around 10-12 minutes, or until it tastes tender. Remove from the heat and set aside to cool, fluffing with a fork.

Make the dressing by whisking together, in a large bowl, the lemon juice, olive oil, crushed garlic clove and honey. Deseed and dice the tomatoes, then add them to the dressing. Chop the herbs and spring onions finely and add them to the dressing, before stirring through the quinoa. Season with salt and freshly ground black pepper, according to taste. Transfer the salad to a serving platter and scatter over the goji berries.

Parsley tempura

A refreshing twist on a Japanese classic, perfect for serving as canapés.

Ingredients:

150g tempura flour mix

150ml sparkling water

Half a teaspoon of paprika

6 sprigs of parsley, with 1cm of stalk left

Rock salt

Vegetable oil, for deep frying

Method:

Add oil to a deep fat fryer, or fill a wok to one third full with vegetable oil, and heat to 180C. Mix together the water, paprika and flour and dip the parsley springs into the mixture. Deep-fry them until the tempura batter turns golden. Drain them on kitchen paper, scatter lightly with salt and serve straight away.

Parsley sauce

Serve this sauce with new potatoes, broad beans and ham or gammon to recreate a classic early summer dish.

Ingredients:

100g flour

100g butter

700ml milk

A big bunch of parsley (curly is best)

Salt and freshly ground black pepper

Method:

Chop the parsley finely and set it to one side. Melt the butter in a saucepan, add the flour to make a roux and stir until its smooth and thickened. Whisk in the milk, a little at a time, being careful to ensure that the sauce doesn't catch on the bottom of the pan. Add a little ham stock if you have cooked it yourself to add extra flavour. Once you have achieved the desired consistency, add salt and pepper to taste then – just before serving – stir in the parsley.

Rosemary baked beans

A vegetarian meal in itself, or a tasty accompaniment to meat.

Ingredients:

1 tbsp olive oil

2 shallots

1 tsp finely chopped rosemary leaves

2 garlic cloves, crushed

1x400g can of chopped tomatoes

125ml chicken stock

1x400g can of flageolet beans

1 tbsp chopped parsley

Salt and pepper

Method:

Chop the shallots finely, heat the olive oil in a frying pan, then fry the shallots for 2-3 minutes until softened. Add the garlic and rosemary and fry for a further 2 minutes. Stir in the chopped tomatoes, heat until boiling (stirring often to avoid burning), add the stock and the drained and rinsed beans, simmering for ten minutes, until the sauce has slightly thickened. Stir in the parsley and seasoning, to taste, before serving.

Apple, blackberry and rosemary crumble

The flavour of rosemary really enhances the fruit in this classic dessert.

Ingredients:

225g blackberries

900g cooking apples (preferably Bramley)

2 sprigs of rosemary

The zest and juice of one large orange

30g sugar

A dash of water

120g plain flour

60g sugar

60g butter, cut into small pieces

Method:

Peel and core the apples and cut into large chunks. Place them in an ovenproof dish and mix in the orange zest and juice, and the blackberries. Bruise the rosemary sprigs and, together with the sugar and water, scatter them over the apples.

Preheat the oven to 200C. In a bowl, rub together the butter and flour with your fingertips, then mix through the sugar. Sprinkle the crumble mixture over the fruit and bake in the oven for 20 minutes. Serve with cream or custard.

Sage palmiers

Easy to make and perfect as canapés.

Ingredients:

A small handful of fresh sage leaves

200g puff pastry (ready made)

1 tbsp of olive oil

8 tbsp fresh parmesan, grated

1 egg

Black pepper, freshly ground

Method:

Heat the olive oil over a medium heat in a frying pan. Add the sage leaves and fry for 1-2 minutes until crispy. Remove with a slotted spoon and place on kitchen paper.

On a lightly floured work surface, roll out the puff pastry into a rectangle, measuring roughly 20cm x 30cm. Sprinkle the parmesan, sage leaves and a scattering of black pepper over the puff pastry, before rolling up the puff pastry, starting at both short ends so that they meet in the middle. Brush the outside of the pastry with beaten egg and chill for half an hour.

Preheat the oven to 200C, take out the pastry, brush it again with beaten egg, then cut it into around 10 slices. Place the slices onto a baking sheet lined with greaseproof paper or silicone and bake for around 10 minutes, until the pastry is puffy and golden brown.

Leave to cool slightly, then serve.

Spicy sage and butternut mash

A healthy variation on mashed potato.

Ingredients:

10 fresh sage leaves

1.5kg butternut squash

40g parmesan

60g butter

A large pinch of chilli flakes

6 tbsp crème fraîche

Salt and pepper

Method:

Chop the sage leaves and peel and cube the butternut squash. Melt the butter in a lidded saucepan and fry the sage in it for around one minute. Stir in the chilli flakes and cubes of butternut, cover the pan with a lid, and cook on a low heat for around 20 minutes, stirring every now and then.

Mash the squash lightly with a fork, then add in the crème fraîche and parmesan, stirring until thoroughly combined. Season with salt freshly ground pepper, according to your taste.

Tarragon chicken with asparagus

This fresh-tasting dish goes very well with new potatoes.

Ingredients:

4 chicken breasts, skinless

1 tbsp olive oil

1 large onion

2 garlic cloves

350ml chicken stock

A small bunch of tarragon

3 tbsp of crème fraîche

Method:

Heat the olive oil in a frying pan, add the onion, garlic and chicken, and cook for five minutes until the onion has softened and the chicken is lightly browned. Turn the chicken during cooking. Pour the stock into the pan, add two sprigs of tarragon, and simmer for five minutes. Turn the chicken before adding the asparagus and cooking for three minutes more.

Chop the rest of the tarragon and stir it through the pan together with the crème fraîche. Heat gently before serving.

Mushroom and tarragon cream

Use this as a filling for vol-au-vents for a perfect pre-dinner appetiser.

Ingredients:

2 shallots

450g chestnut mushrooms

25g butter

A small bunch of tarragon leaves

Madeira

200ml double cream

Method:

Finely chop the shallots and mushrooms and fry them in the butter. Chop the tarragon leaves and add them to the mixture together with a splash of Madeira, salt and freshly ground black pepper, according to taste. Add the cream and allow the mixture to cook gently until reduced by a third.

Fill vol-au-vent cases with the mixture and garnish with chives.

Vegetable soup with thyme and chorizo

A warming and hearty soup, suitable for any occasion. Omit the chorizo if cooking for vegetarians.

Ingredients:

1 leek

1 large carrot

1 sweet potato

1 celery stalk

1 tbsp olive oil

1 tsp ground cumin

1x400g can chopped tomatoes

2 tbsp balsamic vinegar

A small bunch of thyme

150g green beans

570ml vegetable stock

110g raw chorizo sausage

Salt and freshly ground black pepper

Method:

Cut the leek, carrot, potato and celery into small chunks. In a large pan, heat the olive oil and fry the vegetables in it for round 10 minutes, until they are softened but not coloured. Tie the bunch of thyme with string and add it to the pan, together with the cumin, stock, balsamic vinegar, tomatoes and green beans. Simmer for 40 minutes or so on a low heat, until the vegetables are tender.

Chop the chorizo into small chunks and fry until crisp and golden brown. Remove the thyme from the soup and add the chorizo, adjusting the seasoning.

Serve with crusty bread.

Warm potato salad with thyme and shallot dressing

Perfect as a barbeque accompaniment, this fresh and tasty salad has a light and fragrant dressing.

Ingredients:

24 new potatoes

120ml olive oil

4 shallots, finely chopped

8 sprigs of thyme

Summer salad leaves, of your choice

Method:

Bring a pan of water to the boil, add salt and the new potatoes. Cook for around 15 minutes, or until the potatoes feel tender. Drain and allow to cool slightly.

Heat 40ml of the olive oil in a pan and fry the shallot until it's transparent. Add the vinegar and bubble away until the mixture has reduced by half. Take the pan off the heat, strip the thyme leaves from the stalks and add them to the pan, together with the remaining olive oil, stirring thoroughly.

Chop the potatoes in half and scatter over a serving dish. Toss the salad leaves in a little of the dressing, drizzling the rest over the potatoes. Top the potatoes with the dressed salad leaves, and enjoy!

Made in the USA
Middletown, DE
17 November 2016